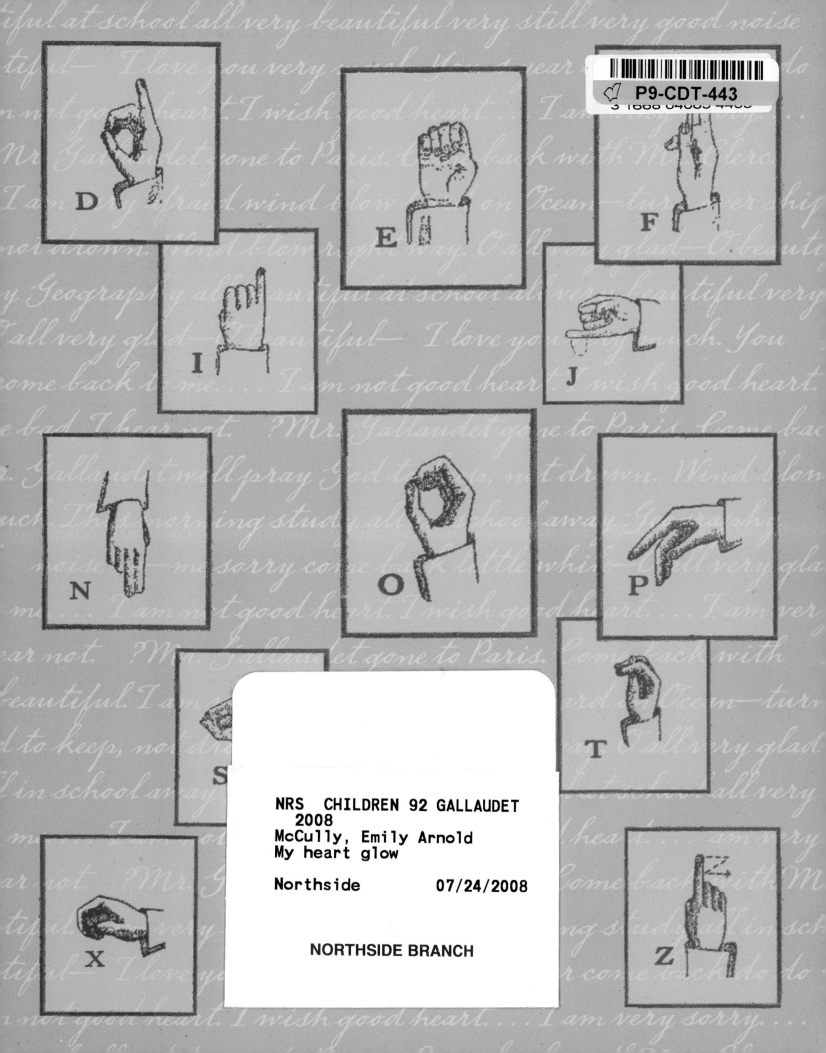

For Nat

My Heart Glow

ALICE COGSWELL, THOMAS GALLAUDET, and the BIRTH of AMERICAN SIGN LANGUAGE

EMILY ARNOLD McCULLY

HYPERION BOOKS FOR CHILDREN

NEW YORK

An Imprint of Disney Book Group

$\mathcal{A}$lice Cogswell watched the children race around the garden one day in 1814. She had tried to join their game, but it was hopelessly confusing to her. Alice was deaf. She had been unable to hear or to speak since she was two. She had nearly died then from the Spotted Fever.

Alice knew that eventually her sisters, Elizabeth and Mary, would come and ask, using the finger signs they had worked out, what she wanted for tea. Her family could nearly always tell what she wanted, but never what she was thinking. I can see out, Alice thought, but no one can see in.

Alice had noticed the young man who stood watching her. Thomas Gallaudet's family lived next door. He had studied to be a preacher. He hoped to work among American Indian tribes and learn their sign language. Now he couldn't take his eyes off Alice's glowing, intelligent face. Yet she looked so alone. He wondered if he could teach her.

He approached, careful not to startle her. Alice smiled up at his kind face. He set his hat on the ground, picked up a stick, and scratched the letters H A T in the sand. He put his hat next to them. Did she see? Alice nodded. In another spot he scratched the letters again. He gestured, and Alice moved the hat to the new letters. She understood!

Gallaudet pantomimed reading a book. Did she want to do that?

Oh, yes! How she longed to read!

He nodded. You shall!

That evening, Gallaudet told Alice's father that she was capable of reading.

"You offer our first hope!" Dr. Cogswell said. "I had feared that without language, her mind was lost."

"Oh, no," Gallaudet said. "Her mind is keen. We need to find a way to nourish it."

Gallaudet began teaching Alice in the afternoons, while her sisters were at school. She made slow progress, learning the alphabet, then simple words. She waited eagerly for Gallaudet every day. She felt as if the lessons had pulled her from a kind of tomb. No one had understood before that she wanted to learn!

But Gallaudet soon realized that teaching words letter by letter would leave them both frustrated. He didn't know how to help her to express thoughts.

One day Dr. Cogswell said, "Alice is not the only deaf child in America. We need a school where she and others like her can be taught."

"I agree with you," Gallaudet said.

"I have read that such schools exist in Great Britain and Europe. Someone has to go there and learn the best method of instruction." Dr. Cogswell paused. "Will you do it, Thomas?"

Gallaudet was startled. He had already chosen his life's work. But teaching little Alice seemed to have changed everything.

"Your child's bright spirit moves me very much," he said. "For her sake, I will go."

Using finger spelling and pantomime, Gallaudet told Alice what he and her father had planned. She understood that her lessons were ending because he was going someplace far away on a ship. For Alice it was a terrifying idea, and she begged him not to go. But he was going for her sake, Gallaudet assured her. He was going to find a better way to teach her. While he was away, just for one year, she must continue to study. He thought she could go to Miss Huntley's school along with her sisters.

Alice was torn. It was thrilling to think of going to school. But ocean voyages were very dangerous. A year was such a long time.

"It will pass quickly if you write letters to me. And I will answer them!" he promised.

Miss Huntley sat her new pupil right beside her own desk. Lessons whirled around Alice—geography, history, literature, mathematics. Not understanding them didn't discourage her. Instead, she told herself that someday, when Mr. Gallaudet came back, she would have a way to learn all those things too.

Then I scrounge a couple of cinnamon buns at the Sidewalk Café and catch up on the news.

I race across the street to the library and e-mail *Ask Queenie.*

To: qdog@weeklybone.dog
From: emmadog@mutts.dog
Subject: George

Dear Queenie,

I'm a pup with a problem. My human, George, barks way too much. It's "Bad! Bad! Bad!" all day long. The least little thing sets him off. He's really getting on my nerves. What should I do? Please answer quickly!

Sincerely,
A desperate dog

I don't have to wait long for an answer.

So I try to make George feel better.

I would have been better off taking a nap on the couch.

Late that night, when I'm sure George is asleep, I use his computer to e-mail *Ask Queenie* for more advice.

To: qdog@weeklybone.dog
From: emmadog@mutts.dog
Subject: GEORGE!

Dear Queenie,

I am the most unappreciated dog in the world. I tried to make George feel better, but your advice didn't work at all. It's still "Bad! Bad! Bad!" all day long.

Yours truly,
An unappreciated dog

P.S. He even called me useless!

To: emmadog@mutts.dog
From: qdog@weeklybone.dog
Subject: GEORGE!

Dear Unappreciated,

USELESS!? My paw! You must show George he can't live without you. Do you help around the house? Do you keep an eye on things? Do you live up to your canine responsibilities? If so, you needn't worry.

Keep that tail wagging!

Queenie

I admit I don't keep an eye on things as much as I should. So that night I decide to be extra-vigilant.

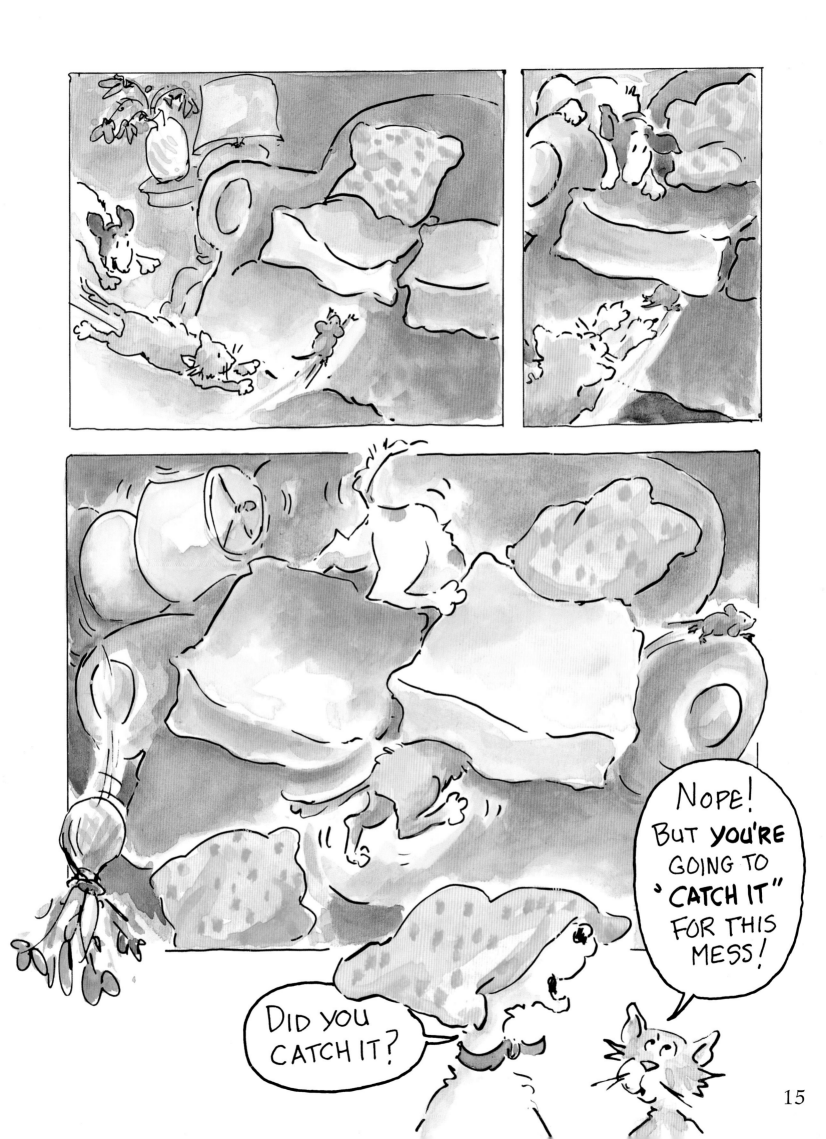

15

Unfortunately, the cat has a point.

But I'm not fast enough!

I'm in real trouble now!

As soon as the library opens, I e-mail
Ask Queenie for more advice.

To: qdog@weeklybone.dog
From: emmadog@mutts.dog
Subject: You-Know-Who

Dear Queenie,

I'm the most misunderstood dog in the world. I did my best to keep an eye on things around the house. But did I get any thanks for my efforts? NO! It's just "Bad! Bad! Bad!" Not even a pat on the head! From now on, I'm going to be like the cat and just nap on the couch all day long.

Yours truly,
Misunderstood

To: emmadog@mutts.dog
From: qdog@weeklybone.dog
Re: You-Know-Who

Dear Misunderstood,

A famous sheepdog once said, "What every dog needs is a job! There are far too many dogs in this world who lie around on the couch waiting for the next free meal." I couldn't agree more! There are many interesting jobs listed in the *Weekly Bone.* A new career will get you off the couch and away from George's tirades.

Keep that tail wagging,
Queenie

Luckily, the library has a copy of the *Weekly Bone.* I flip to the want ads.

Guard dog — German Shepherd preferred.

Airport sniffer — Only German Shepherds or Golden Retrievers need apply.

Actor — Mutt preferred. Amiable disposition required. Should enjoy lying on the couch and must be able to travel. Auditions for *On the Couch* today at 10.

ACTOR! THAT'S THE JOB FOR ME!

I hurry over to the theater. Several dogs are already waiting in line.

ON the COUCH

NEXT, PLEASE!

AUDITIONS HERE →

By the time it's my turn to audition, I'm pretty nervous.

They ask me to:

Dance,

Roll over,

Sing,

And lie on the couch.

They are so impressed with my skills, they give me the job!

But there's a problem. Within hours, I'm on a bus with my fellow actors, speeding away from home, the cat, and George.

Each night we perform in a different town.

I'm a BIG hit! But I can't stop thinking about George.

Finally, after several weeks on the road, we return to perform *On the Couch* in my hometown. I scramble off the bus. We only have a short time to get ready. Then I notice the "Missing" posters.

That night I give my best performance ever.

As we're taking our bows, I hear a familiar voice.

We promise I'll return the next day, and then George and I head home.

We stop for gas.

But, then, of course, there's a problem.

For some reason, George can't open the truck door.

It's more than my tired brain can deal with. I need something to chew to calm my fraying nerves.

The kind of
greens make you
want to be Somebody.

Daddy says he got the
grays.

The straight
shoelaces,
coffee in the car
grays.

The lines
between his eyes,
lookin' at his watch
grays.

FINE
$50

The don't ask for a new skateboard
till tomorrow grays.

Poor Daddy.

NO PARKING
FROM

Sasha says she got the
pinks.

The shiny tights,
ballet after school,
glitter on her cheeks pinks.

The where's my butterfly
hair clip? pinks.

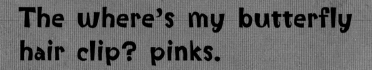

The kind of pinks
make me
want to catch the next bus.

Talia says she got the **indigos.**

I said, indigo's the same as blue.

Talia says, uh-uh,
she got the saxophone
in the subway
indigos.

The hair hangin' loose,
write a poem that don't rhyme indigos.

The kind of indigos
make her act
like the drapes.

Gram's got the **yellows,**
I can tell.

The hummin' that parade song,
flower house slipper yellows.

The mix up some
oatmeal raisin cookies
                    (I hope)
yellows.

Mama
says
she
got
the
reds.

Look out!

Yeah, yesterday I had the
blues.

Today I got the
greens.

Tomorrow maybe it'll be the
silvers.

The rocket-powered skateboard silvers!

And around here, that's okay.
'Cause together we got somethin'
that'll never change.

We got a family—
the kind of family makes you feel
like it's

all

golden.